SOME DAYS YOU JUST HAVE TO CREATE YOUR OWN SUNSHINE

Where there is **woman**, there is *magic*.

Forget safety.
Live where you fear to live.
Destroy your reputation.
BE NOTORIOUS.

Jalaluddin Rumi

**Put on your
positive pants**

Always be a
work in progress

Emily Lillian

You are the universe in ecstatic motion.

Stop acting so small.

Jalaluddin Rumi

If the plan
doesn't work,
change the plan,
never the goal.

Life is tough, but so are you.

Whatever you do or dream
you can do – begin it.
Boldness has genius and
power and magic in it.

Ludwig van Beethoven

Stay classy, sassy . . .   and a bit **bad-assy.**

Imperfection is beauty, madness is genius and it's better to be absolutely ridiculous than absolutely boring.

Marilyn Monroe

Well-behaved women
seldom make history

Laurel Thatcher Ulrich

GROW
THROUGH
WHAT
YOU
GO
Through

Coffee in one hand,

confidence in the other.

She was born to ride unicorns

. . . though she be but little, **she is** *fierce*.

William Shakespeare

People who are truly strong lift others up. People who are truly powerful bring others together.

Michelle Obama

Start each
day with a
grateful heart

You can waste your life drawing lines.

—

Or you can live your life crossing them.

Shonda Rhimes

Show up.

Stand up.

Step up.

NEVER COMPLAIN NEVER EXPLAIN

Katharine Hepburn

#believeandbeawesome

Hug harder.

Laugh louder.

Smile bigger.

Love longer.

The only way to have a friend is to be one

Ralph Waldo Emerson

Don't count
the days.
Make the
days count.

Muhammad Ali

The comeback is always stronger than the setback

Be *yourself*. Everyone else is already taken.

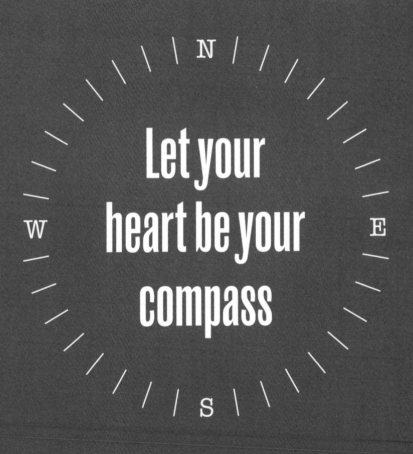

It will never be perfect,

but perfect is overrated.

Perfect is boring.

Tina Fey

WAKE UP.
KICK ASS.
REPEAT.

Never be **limited** by other people's **limited** imaginations

Mae Jemison

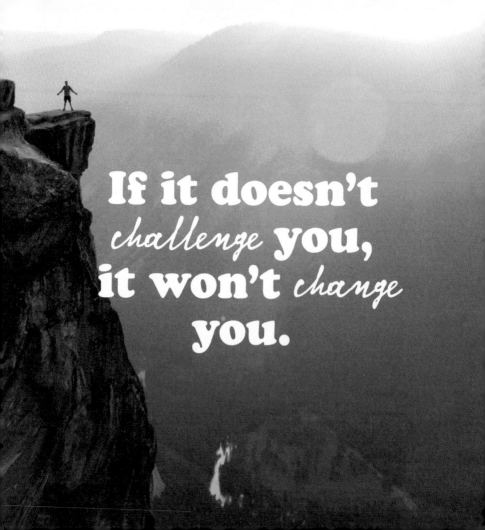

**Start by doing what is necessary;
then do what is possible; and suddenly
you are doing the impossible.**

St Francis of Assisi

DIVAS
don't do
DRAMA.
We do business.

The question isn't who is going to let me; it's **who is going to stop me.**

The greater the storm, the brighter the rainbow.

I am
stronger
than this challenge.
And this challenge
is making me
STRONGER.

Since when was genius

found respectable?

Elizabeth Barrett Browning

Be anything
but predictable

WHEN I'M GOOD,
I'M VERY GOOD,
BUT WHEN
I'M BAD,
I'M BETTER.

Mae West

Don't look back.
The future is forward.

When the whole world is silent, even one voice becomes **POWERFUL.**

Malala Yousafzai

Chin up, princess, or the crown slips.

Life's perfect moments are now

Normal is nothing more than a cycle on a washing machine

Whoopi Goldberg

POWER IS NOT GIVEN TO YOU. YOU HAVE TO TAKE IT.

Beyoncé Knowles

Nothing
changes
if nothing
changes

She needed a

HERO

...so that's what she became.

DON'T BE PUSHED BY YOUR PROBLEMS. BE LED BY YOUR DREAMS.

Ralph Waldo Emerson

It's better to walk alone
than with a crowd going in
the wrong direction

Diane Grant

BE A PINEAPPLE

Stand tall, wear a crown and be sweet on the inside.

Kind **heart.**

Fierce **mind.**

Brave **spirit.**

Don't live life in the past lane

Samantha Ettus

Sunshine mixed with
a little *hurricane*

Brad Paisley & Lee Thomas Miller

The best
way to
predict
the future
is to
create it

Abraham Lincoln

ro stop until you're proud. Don't stop un
til you're proud. Don't stop until you're
n't stop until you're proud. Don't stop u
ı're proud. Don't stop until you're proud
p until you're proud. Don't stop until yo
ud. Don't stop until you're proud. Don't
p until you're proud. Don't stop until yo
ud. Don't stop until you're proud. Don't
til you're proud. Don't stop until you're
n't stop until you're proud. Don't stop u
ı're proud. Don't stop until you're proud
p until you're proud. Don't stop until yo
ud. **Don't stop until you're proud.**

It's okay to be a glowstick.

Sometimes we have to break

before we can shine.

CARPE the heck out of this DIEM

You are far too smart

to be the only thing

standing in your way

What would you do if you weren't afraid?

Sheryl Sandberg

Everything has beauty
but not everybody sees it

Jennifer Lawrence

Throw *glitter* in today's face

Be a *Froot Loop*
in a world of
Cheerios

IN THE END, IT'S NOT GOING TO MATTER HOW MANY BREATHS YOU TOOK, BUT HOW MANY MOMENTS TOOK YOUR BREATH AWAY.

Shing Xiong

When something bad happens,
you have three choices. You can let
it define you, let it destroy you or
let it strengthen you.

Believe in your inner Beyoncé

It's never too late to be what you might have been

George Eliot

LOVE IS NOT WHAT YOU SAY.
LOVE IS WHAT YOU DO.

Make

today

magical

Knowledge is always the loudest voice

Zendaya

Beauty begins the moment you decide to be *yourself*

Coco Chanel

Be your own guru

I'm not weird,

I'm a limited edition.

~~Don't talk~~, ACT.

~~Don't say~~, SHOW.

~~Don't promise~~, PROVE.

What you seek is
seeking you

Never love anyone who treats you like you're or_di_{na}r_y

Oscar Wilde

When it rains, look for rainbows.

When it's dark, look for stars.

The
sun
will
rise
again,
and
so
will
we.

Slay your own dragons, princess.

Passion is the bridge that takes you from pain to change

Frida Kahlo

A [SECOND] SECOND CHANCE DOESN'T MEAN ANYTHING IF YOU HAVEN'T LEARNED FROM THE FIRST MISTAKE

Why be moody

when you can

shake

your booty?

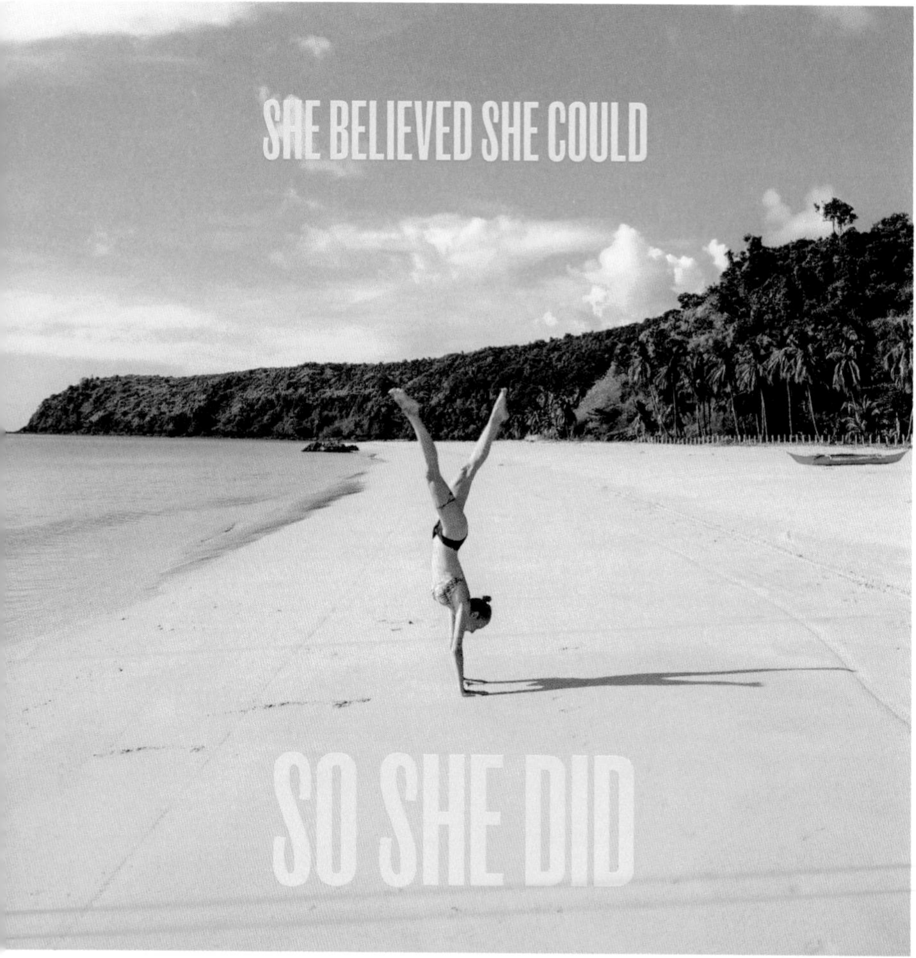
SHE BELIEVED SHE COULD
SO SHE DID

Doing what you like is freedom. Liking what you do is happiness.

Frank Tyger

Throw me to the wolves

and I will return leading the pack

Seneca

BE SO GOOD THEY CAN'T IGNORE YOU

Steve Martin

The impossible
is not a fact:
it's an opinion.

We do not need magic to
transform our world.
We carry all of the
power we need inside
ourselves already.

J.K. Rowling

I haven't failed,

I've found 10,000 ways

that don't work.

Thomas Edison

Beauty
is letting
yourself live

Emma Watson

Difficult roads often lead to beautiful destinations

Make sure you're courageous:
be **strong**, be **kind**, and above all be **humble.**

Serena Williams

Actually . . .

I CAN.

She turned her **can'ts** into **cans** and her **dreams** into **plans**

If you stumble
make it part
of the dance

Don't ever let a soul in the world tell you that you can't be exactly who you are

Lady Gaga

FAILURE IS A BRUISE NOT A TATTOO

Jon Sinclair

Collect moments, not things

are looking at the stars.

but some of us

We are all in the gutter,

Oscar Wilde

ACTION CURES FEAR

**Talk to yourself like you would
to someone you love**

Brené Brown

Every day may not be good

but there is good in every day

All good things are wild and free

Henry David Thoreau

Just wing it.

Life,

eyeliner,

everything.

People say that you're going the wrong way when it's simply a way of your own

Angelina Jolie

You must learn a new way to **think** before you learn a new way to **be**

Leave a *little* sparkle wherever you go

Make it
happen